To Parents and Teachers:

We hope you and the children will enjoy reading this story in English and Spanish. It is simply told, but not *simplified,* so that both versions are quite natural. However, there is lots of repetition for practicing pronunciation, for helping develop memory skills, and for reinforcing comprehension.

At the back of the book, there is a simple picture dictionary with key words as well as a basic pronunciation guide to the whole story.

Here are a few suggestions for using the book:

• First, read the story aloud in English to become familiar with it. Treat it like any other picture book. Look at the drawings, talk about the story, the characters, and so on.

• Then look at the picture dictionary and repeat the key words in Spanish. Make this an active exercise. Ask the children to say the words out loud instead of reading them.

• Go back and read the story again, this time in English and Spanish. Don't worry if your pronunciation isn't quite correct. Just have fun trying it out. If necessary, check the guide at the back of the book, but you'll soon pick up how to say the Spanish words.

• When you think you and the children are ready, try reading the story in Spanish. Ask the children to say it with you. Only ask them to read it if they seem eager to try. The spelling could be confusing and discourage them.

• Above all, encourage the children, and give them lots of praise. They are usually quite unselfconscious, so let them be children and play act, try out different voices, and have fun. This is an excellent way to build confidence for acquiring foreign language skills.

First edition for the United States and Canada published 1996 by Barron's Educational Series, Inc.
Text © Copyright 1996 by b small publishing, Surrey, England
Illustrations © Copyright 1996 by Lucy Keijser
All rights reserved. No part of this book may be reproduced in any form, by photostat, microfilm, xerography, or any other means, or incorporated into any information retrieval system, electronic or mechanical, without the written permission of the copyright owner.
Address all inquiries to: Barron's Educational Series, Inc., 250 Wireless Boulevard, Hauppauge, New York 11788
International Standard Book Number 0-8120-6582-4   Library of Congress Catalog Card Number 95-51387
Printed in China   6789   9598   987

Happy birthday!

¡Feliz cumpleaños!

Mary Risk
Pictures by Lucy Keijser
Spanish by Rosa Martín

BARRON'S

It's my birthday.

Es mi cumpleaños.

Here are all my friends.
Hi! Hello! Come in, everyone!

Aquí están todos mis amigos.
¡Hola! ¿Qué tal? ¡Entren todos!

All these presents for me?
What a great mask!

Todos estos regalos para mí?
¡Qué máscara tan estupenda!

And I love this dinosaur!

¡Y me encanta este dinosaurio!

Let's blow some bubbles.
They're huge.

Vamos a hacer pompas de jabón.
¡Son enormes! ¿Verdad?

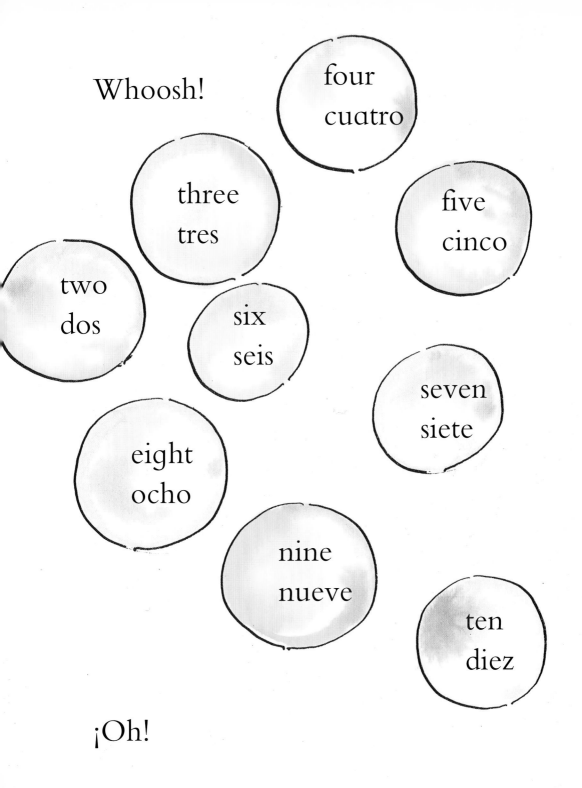

Whoosh!

four
cuatro

three
tres

five
cinco

two
dos

six
seis

seven
siete

eight
ocho

nine
nueve

ten
diez

¡Oh!

Where have they all gone?

¿Dónde se han ido todas?

Oh! Look at Sarah!

¡Oh! ¡Mira a Sara!

Balloons!
Can I have one?

¡Globos!
¿Me das uno?

The red one's for you.
El rojo es para ti.

The green one's for me.
El verde es para mí.

The blue one's for Peter.
El azul es para Pedro.

The purple one's for Clare.
El morado es para Clara.

Oh dear! Good-bye, balloons!

¡Oh, no! ¡Adiós, globos!

Have you lost your balloon?
Never mind, don't cry!

¿Se te ha escapado el globo?
¡No pasa nada! ¡No llores!

Are you hungry?
Have some cake.

¿Tienen hambre?
¡Tomen un poco de pastel!

Are you thirsty?
Have a drink.

¿Tienes sed?
Bebe algo.

That was a lovely party.
Thank you for having us.

Ha sido una fiesta muy bonita.
Gracias por invitarnos.

Look! The balloons!

¡Miren! ¡Los globos!

Good-bye!

¡Adiós!

Pronouncing Spanish

Don't worry if your pronunciation isn't quite correct. The important thing is to be willing to try. The pronunciation guide here is based on the Spanish accent used in Latin America. Although it cannot be completely accurate, it certainly will be a great help:

• Read the guide as naturally as possible, as if it were English.

• Put stress on the letters in *italics* e.g. past*el*.

If you can, ask a Spanish speaking person to help and move on as soon as possible to speaking the words without the guide.

Note: Spanish adjectives usually have two forms, one for masculine and one for feminine nouns. They often look very similar but are pronounced slightly differently, e.g., **divertido** and **divertida** (see the word list below).

Words Las palabras
lahs pah *lah* brahs

happy birthday!
¡feliz cumpleaños!
feh *leehs* koom pleh *ah* nyohs

cake
el pastel
ehl pahs *tehl*

present
el regalo
ehl reh *gah* loh

balloon
el globo

ehl *gloh* boh

bubble
la pompa de jabón

lah *pohm* pah deh hah *bohn*

mask
la máscara

lah *mahs* cah rah

hi, how are you?
¿qué tal?

keh *tahl*

hi/hello
¡hola!

oh lah

dinosaur
el dinosaurio

ehl dee noh *sow* ree oh

thank you
gracias

grah see ahs

goodbye
adiós

ah thee *ohs*

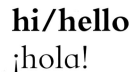

friend
el amigo/la amiga

ehl ah *mee* goh/lah ah *mee* gah

lovely
bonito/bonita
boh *nee* toh/boh *nee* tah

great
estupendo/estupenda
ehs too *pehn* doh/ehs too *pehn* dah

fantastic
fantástico/fantástica
fahn *tahs* tee koh/fahn *tahs* tee kah

fun
divertido/divertida
dee vehr *tee* tho/dee vehr *tee* tha

party
la fiesta
lah fee*ess*ta

red
rojo/roja
roh hoh/*roh* hah

purple
morado/morada
moh *rah* tho/moh *rah* tha

blue
azul
ah *sool*

green
verde
vehr deh

A simple guide to pronouncing this Spanish story

Es mi cumpleaños.
ehs mee koom *pleh ah* nyohs

Aquí están todos mis amigos.
ah *kee* ehs *tahn* toh thohs mees ah *mee* gohs

¡Hola! ¿Qué tal? ¡Entren todos!
oh lah, keh *tahl, ehn* trehn *toh* thos

¿Todos estos regalos para mí?
toh thos *ehs* tohs reh *gah* lohs *pah* rah mee

¡Qué máscara tan estupenda!
keh *mahs* kah rah tahn ehs too *pehn* dah

¡Y me encanta este dinosaurio!
ee meh ehn *kahn* tah *ehs* teh dee noh *sow* ree oh

Vamos a hacer pompas de jabón.
vah mohs ah ah *sehr pohm* pahs deh hah *bohn*

¡Son enormes! ¿Verdad?
sohn eh *norh* mehs, *vehr* dah

una, dos, tres, cuatro, cinco, seis, siete, ocho, nueve, diez, ¡oh!
oo nah, dohs, trehs, *kwah* troh, *seen* koh, seh ees, see *eh* teh, *oh* choh, *noo eh* veh, *dee* ehs, oh

¿Dónde se han ido todas?
dohn deh seh ahn *ee* tho *tho* thas

¡Oh! ¡Mira a Sara!
oh *mee* rah ah *sah* rah

¡Globos!
gloh bohs

¿Me das uno?
meh dahs oo noh

El rojo es para ti.
ehl *roh* hoh ehs *pah* rah tee

El verde es para mí.
ehl *vehr* deh ehs *pah* rah mee

El azul es para Pedro.
ehl ah *sool* ehs *pah* rah *peh* droh

El morado es para Clara.
ehl moh *rah* tho ehs *pah* rah *clah* rah

¡Es fantástico!
ehs fahn *tahs* tee koh

¡Qué divertido!
keh dee vehr *tee* tho

¡Oh, no! ¡Adiós, globos!
oh noh ah thee *ohs gloh* bohs

¿Se te ha escapado el globo?
seh teh ah ehs kah *pah* tho ehl *gloh* boh

¡No pasa nada! ¡No llores!
noh *pah* sah *nah* tha, no *yorh* ehs

¿Tienen hambre?
tee eh nen *ahm* breh

Tomen un poco de pastel.
toh mehn oon *poh* koh deh pahs *tehl*

¿Tienes sed?
tee eh nehs sehd

Bebe algo.
beh beh *ahl* goh

Ha sido una fiesta muy bonita.
ah *see* tho oo nah *fee ehs* tah mwee boh *nee* tah

Gracias por invitarnos.
grasee ahs poor eenveet *ahr* noss

¡Miren! ¡Los globos!
mee rehn lohs *gloh* bohs

¡Adiós!
ah thee *ohs*